# THE FACTS ON
# LIFE
# AFTER
# DEATH

# John Ankerberg
# & John Weldon

HARVEST HOUSE PUBLISHERS
Eugene, Oregon 97402

### Other books by
### John Ankerberg and
### John Weldon

*The Facts on Astrology*
*The Facts on the New Age Movement*
*The Facts on Spirit Guides*
*The Facts on the Masonic Lodge*
*The Facts on the Jehovah's Witnesses*
*The Facts on the Mormon Church*
*The Facts on False Teaching in the Church*
*The Facts on Hinduism in America*
*The Facts on the Occult*
*The Facts on Islam*
*The Facts on Rock Music*
*The Facts on Holistic Health*
*The Facts on UFOs and Other
Supernatural Phenomena*

**THE FACTS ON LIFE AFTER DEATH**

Copyright © 1992 by The Ankerberg
   Theological Research Institute
Published by Harvest House Publishers
Eugene, Oregon 97402

ISBN 0-89081-992-0

**Printed in the United States of America.**

*One of the most consistent findings to emerge from the body of near-death research is that people who have had NDEs [near-death experiences] do not as a rule fear death at all; furthermore, their loss of the fear of death appears to be permanent following an NDE.*

> —Kenneth Ring,
>    *Heading Toward Omega: In
>    Search of the Meaning of the
>    Near-Death Experience* (p. 20)

# *CONTENTS*

## SECTION TWO
### The Cultic View of Death:
### Universalism, Annihilationism and
### Conditional Immortality

## SECTION THREE
### The Biblical View of Death:
### Eternal Heaven or Hell

# The Importance of Death in Modern Society

> Death is one of the few universal experiences of human existence. It is the most predictable event in our lives, one that is to be expected with absolute certainty. Yet, the nature of death is immersed in deep mystery.[1]
> —Stanislav Grof, M.D. and
> Joan Halifax, *The Human Encounter with Death*

Vast numbers of books now exist on dying—books for the terminally ill and their family and friends, for researchers and death educators, for psychotherapists and gerontologists, for physicians, nurses and hospice workers. One would think death were a new topic.

There are also instruction manuals on what to expect and/or what to do at or after death, such as the Tibetan, Egyptian, American, and other Books of the Dead. There are even various New Age devices to help induce "near-death experiences" or "out-of-body experiences" as a "preparation" for death. And there are now even self-help manuals on how to kill yourself.

At numerous universities the social sciences (psychology, for example) frequently incorporate the field of thanatology—the study of death. Some writers have even divided the subject into two major branches—"applied" and "theoretical" thanatology.*

Today, a new interest in death has emerged that promises to expand well into the twenty-first century. Perhaps more than any other subject, the "near-death experience" (NDE) has helped resurrect this interest in death. But what is an NDE? It is an alleged experience of the afterlife that takes place while a person is clinically dead.

It appears that, along with everything else, death has come out of the closet. In the March 1992 *Life* Magazine it was noted that "the increasingly open discussion of these [NDE] visions has begun to change the climate of dying in America."[2]

---

* In applied thanatology one is taught how to die "correctly" according to various Eastern/occult traditions—typically utilizing the Books of the Dead. These books are often incorporated with the latest findings in parapsychology and similar research into the Near-Death Experience (NDE).

The theoretical branch principally involves the study of the "evidence" for survival after death—which includes not only NDEs, but mediumism, reincarnation research, out-of-body episodes, poltergeists and apparition research, and many other occult topics.

# SECTION ONE

## The Near-Death Experience Popularizing an Occultic View of Death

### 1. What is a near-death experience?

The typical near-death experience (NDE) has been described by leading death researcher Dr. Raymond Moody. His several books, including the eight million bestseller *Life After Life*, opened a new era of "scientific" study of the near-death experience. With the near-death or clinical death phenomenon some people who are brought back from "death" have reported being alive the entire time they were "dead." This phenomenon occurs among people with a wide diversity of religious belief and no religious belief at all—from atheists to Zen Buddhists.[3]

When co-author John Weldon wrote his first book on the subject in 1976, there was almost no literature available. Today there are scores of books and research papers. Unfortunately, almost all of them reveal that the NDE is frequently an occult experience.

The composite or classic NDE* involves the perception of being "out of the body"—and looking down at one's body while resuscitation attempts are being administered. Soon afterward the person finds he or she is in another location

---

\* The reader should understand that approximately 65 percent of those who have been clinically dead report no experience at all. Further, those who have experienced a near-death episode report experiences along a continuum.[4] Only infrequent or rare experiences include the "composite" or "full" NDE containing almost all the characteristics noted to date in NDEs. The "normal" and most frequent NDE contains some or many but not all the characteristics of the "composite" experience. The "deep" NDE is also not a composite experience. But in its large number of characteristics and/or its profundity (including the subsequent impact upon the person), it is distinguished as a more powerful NDE than average and in some respects is as powerful as the full-blown occult NDE. We should remember that not every NDE is by definition occult. Nevertheless, the more pagan a culture becomes, the more it opens itself to occult forces.

In our opinion, the spiritual background of those having deep NDEs could where the spirit world is encountered. There the person engages in non-verbal or verbal communication with various spirits, usually of dead friends and relatives or a "being of light." This entity is often very warm and loving and involves the "dead" person in an evaluation of his or her life by showing an instantaneous playback of the major events. At some point, the person finds himself approaching a barrier or border which he is not allowed to cross. He is told he must go back to earth, for his time to die has not yet arrived. However, the participant's experience in this other state of existence is frequently so peaceful, joyful, and loving that he desperately does not want to return. Nevertheless, he finds himself back in his body anyway. And when he awakens in this world he finds that he had been pronounced dead, but was fortunately (?) revived.[6]

Skeptics and materialists are doubtful about all this and have put forth a variety of theories that they think explain the phenomenon. Some of the major explanations are that NDEs are (1) hallucinations induced by pain or medication; (2) leftover memories from the experience of birth; (3) the brain's reaction to altered levels of carbon dioxide; (4) psychological wish fulfillment (the hope of a heaven); (5) experiences related to Jung's theory of the collective unconscious and/or archetypes; (6) experiences induced by drugs—LSD, heroin, marijuana, etc., or various anesthetic agents; (7) temporal lobe seizures, and (8) sensory deprivation.

The problem with these theories is that none of them adequately explain the facts of the NDE. For example, they cannot explain how people who were brain dead at the time are later able to describe in vivid detail the attempts of medical personnel to resuscitate them. It would seem that the most logical explanation is that these people were somehow outside their bodies actually observing the procedure.

Let us give an example. In one study, 25 medically informed patients were asked to make educated guesses

---

prove significant. Examining their family histories to four generations in terms of psychic/occult involvement—or even a distinctly anti-Christian orientation—may help reveal the origin of these experiences. Deeper NDEs are occult experiences, and occult experiences frequent persons for specific reasons based on specific spiritual conditions.[5]

Nevertheless, if even 10 percent of the ten million people who have had the "average" NDE have had a deep NDE, we are dealing with over one million persons who have had the fully transformative NDE experience. Furthermore, as our technology improves and resuscitation attempts continue, there will be millions more, so none can deny the importance of this phenomenon. The fact that this experience itself (unsought and unexpected) may finally produce occult transformation in the lives of several *million* persons is substantiated by the occult revival now coursing through society.

about what happens when a doctor attempts to resuscitate a clinically dead patient. Almost all persons in the control group (23 of 25) made "major mistakes" in providing descriptions of the resuscitation procedure. On the other hand, "none of the near-death patients made mistakes in describing what went on in their own resuscitations."[7] Studies like this present evidence that these people were actually outside their bodies looking down upon their "death" just as they claimed.

## 2. How frequent are these experiences? What are their implications?

It should be emphasized that not every dying person has an experience of this type. Most have none at all, and of those who do, not all are glorious. Although most Americans seem unaware of the fact, many people—perhaps up to half—report hellish experiences (see Q. 12). Further, Christian and non-Christian NDEs appear to be of a qualitatively different nature; for instance, the occult elements are typically lacking in the Christian NDE.[8]

However, polls indicate that some ten million Americans have had a near-death experience, and the influence of these experiences upon the public's perception of death has been dramatic. The NDE has played a major role in promoting the view that death may not be so bad after all. Further, millions of NDEs have helped to undergird an occult view of death (and even life) as something that is highly positive. For example, contacting the alleged dead or other spirits is so frequent in the NDE that the disciplines most likely to benefit from such episodes are mediumism, channeling and other forms of spiritism. Thus, if we examine near-death research as a whole, it essentially confirms the mediumistic view of the afterlife. (See Q. 5.)

In fact, as more scientists have become interested in the NDE, the possibility has emerged for a "scientific" necromancy to develop under the guise of death research. Because NDEs often involve contact with the dead, these experiences can be used to promote a "legitimate scientific" basis to study mediumism and other forms of spiritism. After all, some may reason, if *dying* people experience contact with the dead, how can scientific objectivity be retained if we refuse to study *living* contact with the dead—for example, through mediumism and other forms of the occult?

Nevertheless, Gallup and other polls consistently reveal that over 70 percent of Americans believe in life after death, and have since 1944 when surveys began: 70 to 80 percent continue to believe in heaven and 50 to 60 percent in hell.*[9]

But with the occult revival in our culture, necromancy has also been increasingly accepted. Almost half of a Los Angeles sample (44 percent) "claimed encounters with others known to be dead."[10] A nationwide poll conducted in 1986 by sociologist Andrew Greeley of the University of Chicago National Opinion Research Center, based on a sample of almost 1500 people, found nearly identical results—42 percent believed they had been in contact with the dead.[11] Perhaps this explains why channeling alone is now a $100 million a year business.[12]

One reason these NDEs are so powerful in our culture is that they seem to deny the biblical teaching of an eternal hell, which many people fear. Rather, these experiences teach people that they will live forever in a heavenly environment and that there are no consequences to death at all. This is what most people want to believe.

Thus, the way the NDE is currently being popularized in American life the biblical concept of hell could be erased from our culture. Millions of people who once weren't so sure are now convinced that death is a wonderful experience and that there is no hell.[13] Even many ministers have been so influenced by the near-death experience as to reject the biblical view and adopt an occult one. All of this is a reflection of our cultural swing toward the New Age view of death, which is fundamentally spiritistic in nature.

## 3. Is the NDE a genuine experience with death or merely a mystical experience with profound consequences?

What many people do not understand is that with an NDE we are not dealing with true death. And, we are certainly not dealing in the realm of scientific confirmation of life after death, despite some proponents' claims. Rather, we are encountering personal, mystical/occult *experiences* that occur in some near-death states. But these same experiences also occur in many occult religions and practices and in various altered states of consciousness wholly unrelated to death per se.

For example, in large measure the NDE is merely one form of the occult out-of-body experience (OBE). Both have fundamentally the same impact on the person—removal of the fear of death and dramatic psychological aftereffects.[14]

---

* Although over half believed in hell, only 3 to 4 percent thought their chances were good of going there.

But both the NDE and OBE have many other similarities including cross-cultural occurrence, spiritistic contacts, worldview changes and development of psychic powers.[15]

One of the leading modern NDE researchers is University of Connecticut psychologist Dr. Kenneth Ring. In *Heading Toward Omega*, he reveals two crucial implications of the NDE: (1) its removal of the fear of death; and (2) its radical transformation of the living.

For almost everyone Ring and other researchers have encountered, the NDE has been one of utterly indescribable joy, love, beauty, peace, and harmony. According to Ring, "The great unanimity of these reports means that there is a consensus among near-death experiencers concerning what it is like to die.... The experience of death is exceedingly pleasant. Indeed, the word 'pleasant' is far too mild; the word 'ecstatic' would be chosen by many survivors of this experience. No words are truly adequate to describe the sense of ultimate perfection that appears to characterize the entry into death."[16]

He cites the description given by the famed psychotherapist Carl Jung who described the feelings he had after his own NDE: "What happens after death is so unspeakably glorious that our imaginations and our feelings do not suffice to form even an approximate conception of it...."[17] Thus Ring concludes: "No one who has experienced, even vicariously, what NDErs have can ever again regard death with anything other than a sense of infinite gratitude for its existence. This, I submit, is what follows from a careful perusal of near-death experiences, but what follows from a study of *aftereffects* is different—and just as profound. It is nothing less than a new view of life."[18]

In essence, the NDE itself is analogous to the planting of a spiritual "seed" within a person which then appears to grow into its genetically predetermined tree—replete with fruit. As Ring comments, "The key to the meaning of NDEs lies in the study of their aftereffects...."[19]

This is why, Ring says, almost all early researchers necessarily missed the true meaning of the NDE—enough time had not elapsed to examine its real fruit. We agree. By examining the "fruit" of the NDE, we may ascertain its true meaning. In the next several questions we will do this.

## 4. Are the "beings of light" and alleged spirits of dead friends and relatives who they claim to be? What do authorities in this area say?

People who encounter the "being of light," "the light" or the alleged spirits of dead friends and relatives in the NDE are profoundly influenced. Many think they have encountered the biblical "God," "Christ," "angels" or the actual human dead. But this could not possibly be true. Why? Because, on the one hand, the entities of the NDE act in ways that are contrary to the purposes of God and Christ as revealed in the Bible. And, on the other hand, the "being of light" and other spirits act in virtually the same manner as the spirits contacted by mediums and spiritists for millennia.

The actions and statements of the "being of light," the "dead," and other spirits indicate they are not Jesus Christ, the human dead or good angels. The "being of light" cannot be Christ because the "being of light" denies Jesus' teachings in the Bible. And Christ cannot deny Himself by rejecting His earlier teachings.[20]

The alleged spirits of the dead cannot be the human dead, for Scripture tells us that the unsaved dead are confined and unable to reach the living, and the saved dead are with Christ (2 Peter 2:9; Luke 16:19-31; Acts 1:25; 2 Corinthians 5:8; Philippians 1:23).

Furthermore, the other spirits cannot be the holy angels because holy angels are sinless beings who would never contradict what God has taught in the Bible.

Biblically, considering the eternal importance of the subject of death as well as the existence of spiritual warfare (Ephesians 6:10-18), it is unlikely all this is coincidental.

The occult messages frequently conveyed by the "being of light" and the alleged spirits of the dead prove that they are lying spirits. They offer the following unbiblical teachings: (1) *Death is something good:* There is no judgment at death; Death equals God equals Love; (2) *There is no hell:* God accepts all men unconditionally irrespective of their beliefs and actions on earth; all men will go to heaven; (3) *The Bible is wrong:* The Christian view of death is false; it is the Eastern/occult view of death that is correct; and (4) *Occult practice is beneficial:* It is important to develop psychic powers; contacting the spirit world is a godly endeavor.[21]

The evidence is compelling that the spirits of the occult are really lying spirits—in other words, demons who impersonate the dead and others in order to deceive people spiritually. That demons not only have legendary cunning, but are also polymorphs—able to change shape at will—is a widely recognized aspect of the occult. This is why many have concluded that those who encounter occult phenomena in the near-death experience are victims of the same deceiving spirits.[22]

This deceitfulness of the spirits is born out in part by the testimony of numerous former mediums and occultists such as Raphael Gasson, Victor Ernest, Johanna Michaelson, Doreen Irvine, Ben Alexander, and others. At one time, such individuals were convinced that their loving and friendly spirit guides, the "beings of light," "dead friends and relatives," "angels," and the "Jesus" they communed with were, in fact, good spirits. But in the end they realized they were only deceiving spirits who had impersonated good spirits in order to lead them astray.[23]

## 5. Does the NDE confirm the occult (mediumistic) view of death and the afterlife?

Another line of evidence suggesting the essential connection between the NDE and occultism is that thousands of mediums, channelers and psychics express the same view about death as represented in the NDE and by the "being of light" and other spirits.

Indeed, as one surveys the content of the "deep" NDE (see Q. 1), one discovers that it confirms the mediumistic view of the afterlife. For example, many persons feel that while they were in "the Light," "all [their] sins were forgiven" and they felt "perfectly and totally free."[24] "The Light," which they mistakenly interpret as God or Christ, may also give them direct telepathic information that fundamentally reflects and inculcates mediumistic philosophy. This includes the following ideas: earth as a "school" for spiritual learning continued after death; liberal theology: the brotherhood of man, the fatherhood of God, the social gospel; Universalism: that all mankind will finally be saved; a denial of the biblical reality and consequence of sin; the importance of individual and planetary occult consciousness transformation and evolution into divinity; a trust in the "ultimate good within us all," and so on.[25]

Of course, if it is lying spirits who promote a mediumistic worldview in the seance, who then is doing it in the NDE?

All this is why many NDE researchers have noted the similarity between the message of the NDE and the message of mediumism. Parapsychologist Dr. Karlis Osis, a leading NDE researcher, observes that the NDE "tends to confirm much of the picture gained through mediumship."[26]

The late D. Scott Rogo was an authority on the paranormal, having authored some 15 books on the subject. After reviewing all the relevant literature and research on near-death experiences from 1882 to the present, he concludes that the findings of the modern near-death researchers only reinforce what the mediums and spiritists have long taught: "Finally, I cannot help but be impressed by how closely the findings of everyone from [Karlis] Osis to [Raymond] Moody match what the Spiritualists [spiritists] of the Victorian age taught about death and the process of dying.... I fail to see that any of the 'discoveries' by Osis, Crookall, Moody, or other researchers differ from what was really discovered and taught by the Spiritualists ages ago."[27]

One of the key early researchers in near-death experiences, Frederick Myers, stated in his famous work, *Human Personality and Its Survival of Bodily Death*, how indebted he was to the spiritualists: "How much I owe to certain observations made by members of this group—how often my own conclusions concur with conclusions at which they have previously arrived."[28]

Mediumistic and other occult views of death frequently stem from personal out-of-body experiences and communication with spirit guides, "ascended masters," etc. For example, the famous eighteenth-century medium Emanuel Swedenborg chronicled many personal experiences from his own out-of-body travels that are identical to the near-death ones described in his 1758 text *Heaven and Its Wonders and Hell*.[29]

Likewise, the world-famous trance medium Arthur Ford had an OBE/near-death experience that was identical almost point for point with the composite NDE experience detailed by Moody and others, as reported in his *The Life Beyond Death*.[30]

Both Swedenborg and Ford founded occult, anti-Christian movements. Swedenborg began his Church of the New Jerusalem, and Ford was responsible for interesting tens of thousands of people in the occult through founding his Spiritual Frontiers Fellowship. In fact, Ford declared he was "sent back" by the spirits for this express mission—to help "remove for all time the fear of death."[31] This goal given to him by the spirits is precisely the personal impact of the modern NDE.

In essence, no one can deny that for many people the NDE is or becomes an occult experience. In fact, if the spirits of the occult routinely confess that they can purposely induce out-of-body experiences in their contacts,[32] why should anyone assume this could never happen in the NDE, especially if a person has previously been involved in the occult, as is frequently true.[33]

In conclusion, in that mediumistic teachings are supported by the "being of light" and the alleged spirits of the dead, we again conclude that they are not who they claim to be.

# 6. Does the NDE undermine the biblical view of salvation?

Not only does the NDE remove the fear of death, but also it simultaneously inhibits biblical repentance and salvation. The biblical concept of sin has little or no relevance to the "Light": "...in most cases, the reward-punishment model of the afterlife is abandoned and disavowed, even by many who had been accustomed to thinking in those terms. They found, much to their amazement, that even when their most apparently awful and sinful deeds were made manifest before the being of light, the being responded not with anger and rage, but rather only with understanding, and even with humor."[34] And when a person becomes convinced of complete acceptance by the Light ("God"), receiving Christ as his or her savior from sin becomes almost irrelevant. For example, one spirit told a person during his NDE, "There are no sins. Not in the way you think about them on earth. The only thing that matters here is how you think."[35]

The warmth of the "being of light" and the feeling of all-accepting love strongly conveys the message that one is accepted and forgiven wholly apart from personal faith in Christ. Thus people who have NDEs, whether in childhood or adulthood, universally lose the fear of death even though they remain non-Christians: "After the event, NDErs no longer fear death.... [and] Fear of hellish punishment for earthly deeds is no longer a problem for many."[36]

Those who have an NDE may also be commanded to disseminate the message that God will save everyone: "Nancy says that the Light told her in these 'exact words': 'With the gift you have now received, go forth and tell the masses of people that life after death exists: that you shall all experience my PROFOUND LOVE.'"[37]

No one can deny that many people are dramatically changed as a result of their NDE. They often become zealous converts to religion. But as we will see later (see Q. 9) the religion they become converted to is not Christian.

One NDEr was told that her new mission was to communicate the particular knowledge given her in the NDE in order to bring a "proper" understanding to mankind concerning the "true" nature of death. She recognized this message was incompatible with biblical teaching and so abandoned her Christian upbringing:

> Stella was raised in a fundamentalist tradition, and yet she still is reluctant to identify the being she saw

as Christ. At this juncture, however, Stella's story takes a most unexpected turn. While communicating telepathically with the being of light, she was told that she was Jewish!...it facilitated the already accelerating process of Stella's awakening to a full realization of her own authentic identity—first suggested to her by the being of light. Since that time there have been many changes in her life. Not only has she formally converted to Judaism (which proved quite a shock to her fundamentalist family) and divorced her husband, but also this formerly shy... woman has become a successful business woman, has served on the White House Council on children and youth, and has become actively involved in local politics.[38]

In essence, the need for biblical salvation is repudiated by many NDEs through the following means: (1) the teaching that death is something good; (2) the trivializing of sin; (3) the strongly communicated perceptions of preexisting divine forgiveness and the experience of an "all encompassing love"; (4) the profundity and authority of the experience itself over "dead" literature such as the Bible; and (5) the tendency toward personal works righteousness found in many experiences, which moves a person toward a kind of "social gospel" wherein the Light ("God") or the experience itself conveys the idea that one must seek good works, the welfare of humanity, the improvement of world conditions, peace and love, and so on.

## 7. How could such peaceful and loving experiences be something spiritually deceptive?

Researchers are fond of pointing out that the NDE and its aftermath are characteristically benign. Not only is the experience itself indescribably wondrous—full of love, peace and joy—but also the results of that experience in a person's life are characteristically good. People become more concerned about other people. They become kinder, gentler, more understanding and compassionate. As Dr. Raymond Moody points out in *The Light Beyond*, "On the whole, the NDE changes a person for the positive....In my twenty years of intensive exposure to NDErs, I have yet to find one who hasn't had a very deep and positive transformation as a result of his experience....All of the scholars and clinicians I have talked to who have interviewed NDErs have come to the same conclusion: they are better people because of their experience."[39]

Most NDErs claim that the result of the experience was to encourage them to love more. "'Have you learned to love?' is a question faced in the course of the episode by almost all NDErs. Upon their return, almost all of them say that love is the most important thing in life. Many say it is why we are here."[40] As "the Light" told one NDEr, "Love is the key to the universe."[41]

So how could such a wonderful experience with such positive results be spiritually evil? Perhaps it would help to remember that there are many things in life that can initially seem wonderful and yet be deceptive or destructive—such as illegal drugs and promiscuous sex. Nor should we forget that the Bible teaches that Satan and his demons can appear as "angels of light" and "servants of righteousness" (2 Corinthians 11:14,15). Finally, in the NDE the content  and meaning of the word "love" must be evaluated. When "the Light" tells people they must love more, what does this mean?

The general teaching that people should "love more"—without specific content to the word love—may be a frequent teaching of the spirits, but it is still not biblical. Unless love is defined biblically (e.g., 1 Corinthians 13; 1 John 3:16; 4:7-15), it does not come from God. Without proper content and action, "love" is a vague emotion or relative belief that has little of lasting value. Even genuine love for other people may be deficient when genuine love for the one true God is lacking.

No one is saying that the NDE isn't often wonderful or that the results aren't in some sense positive. We are only saying that both the experience and the results are fundamentally deceptive from the perspective of biblical teaching. Being kinder, more compassionate, and more loving to others is good. But this does not gain one entrance to heaven. Nor does feeling love for an unidentified "being of light." Only receiving Christ as one's Savior from sin provides entrance into true eternal life (John 1:12; 3:16).

Unfortunately, the positive value changes in most NDErs—more love, more concern for others, a quest for meaning, a more positive self-image—become to varying degrees integrated with an unbiblical worldview. In other words, these positive changes support a fundamentally false spiritual philosophy. Thus, without the biblical corrective, even these positive aspects can become something negative because they undergird a powerful experience that is spiritually misleading.

There is a human tendency, in both researcher and layman alike, to avoid the unpleasantness of death. Dr. John J.

Heaney is Professor of Theology at Fordham University and author of *The Sacred and the Psychic*, a book accepting the integration of Christian theology and the occult. He writes, "I find nothing demonic in NDEs. The effects of the experience satisfy the criteria one looks for in judging the validity and fruitfulness of mystical experience, at least in its broadest sense: a sense of peace and joy, a change of horizon toward the spiritual, a lasting reformation of one's life, and a greater sense of charity and of the need for growth."[42]

But again if the spiritual context in which these events occur is anti-Christian, even the good results can become tainted. What must also be remembered is that pleasantness alone is not always a legitimate criteria for that which is good or true. Indeed, even experiences of outright demon possession *can* be indescribably *pleasant, blissful* and *loving.* Reports from those who have been spirit possessed reveal that demons have the capacity to manipulate the mind quite in the same way drugs do—very powerfully and positively. This is supported by modern American occult testimonies, the research of Malachi Martin in *Hostage to the Devil: The Possession and Exorcism of Five Living Americans,* and in any number of anthropological studies of spirit possession. Mediums, spiritists, channelers and other occultists who describe their possession by spirit beings or spirit guides frequently report loving, blissful, wonderful encounters.[43] That is, after all, what one should expect: if the devil is serious about deceiving people over spiritual truth, he will do what is needed.

What the NDE does is powerfully reinforce a common, if mistaken, theme in modern culture—that God loves all persons unconditionally and will grant everyone entrance into heaven on the basis of their being "good" people. The NDE communicates that God is more concerned with a person's good deeds than He is with their particular religious beliefs. But this is wrong biblically. The Bible teaches that death leads to judgment, not bliss (Hebrews 9:27), and that God is very concerned with what a person believes religiously. In fact, apart from personal belief in the true Christ, no one will enter heaven (John 3:16,36; Acts 4:12; 1 John 5:11-12).

However, because the NDE is so profoundly "spiritual," good and full of loving experiences, the vast majority of people assume that the experience itself must be divine—something from God. But these wonderful experiences lead to theological error: they almost always convey the false assurance of Universalism (that all will be saved at death), and they almost never bring biblical repentance. In other words, they never cause people to see themselves as sinners who need salvation in Christ. But if the primary message God seeks to communicate to men is that they need salvation in Christ (Matthew 28:19-20; 1 Timothy 2:3-7), how could these experiences possibly originate from God? An experience that leads people to reject God's salvation cannot be divine, no matter how pleasant.

All this fits with what the Bible teaches about the nature of spiritual warfare: that spiritual evil commonly imitates that which is good and righteous in order to deceive people concerning the truth of what God has revealed in the Bible. Again, the Apostle Paul wrote in 2 Corinthians 11:14,15 that "even Satan *disguises* himself as an angel of light" and his ministers as "servants of *righteousness*." Therefore, it should surprise no one that the devil can imitate a "being of light" or that his demons frequently do the same.

The following examples prove that the NDE, in spite of its *appearance*, can be something fundamentally deceptive concerning the most important issue in life (personal salvation), and therefore is also something fundamentally evil (1 John 2:18-26).

Moody comments that while NDErs tend to become "spiritual," this does not mean they enter the Church—"to the contrary, they tend to abandon religious doctrine purely for the sake of doctrine."[44] As one NDEr commented, "A lot of people I know are going to be surprised when they find out that the Lord isn't interested in theology."[45] Likewise, after her NDE, a very devout and "doctrine abiding Lutheran" concluded that God "didn't care about church doctrine at all."[46] And a pastor who preached on hell was told by the "being of light" "not to speak to his congregation like this anymore."[47]

Biblically, of course, God *is* interested in doctrine (or theology) because He is a God of truth. The Bible is full of God's commands that His people be very concerned about "correct doctrine" (e.g., Titus 1:9; 1 Timothy 6:3).

But whether the NDEr is a secularist or a religious person before his experience, the end result is the same: "Both groups emerge with an appreciation of religion that is different from the narrowly defined one established by most churches. They come to realize through this experience that religion is not a matter of one 'right' group versus several 'wrong' groups. People who undergo an NDE come out of it saying that religion concerns your ability to love—not doctrines and denominations. In short, they think that God is a much more magnanimous being than they previously thought, and that denominations don't count."[48]

Thus, "What is the basic message that the NDEr comes away with? That knowledge and love are the most important things. It is the formal religions that have added all the dogma and doctrine."[49]

But can gaining more knowledge save people from their sins? And again, who defines what love is? Who places the moral limits on knowledge or love? The spirits?

Either through the verbal instruction of the spirits or by mystical illumination, the NDE teaches people to pursue *knowledge* but to avoid *doctrine*. Unfortunately, this simultaneously opens people to learning the occult while inhibiting their acceptance of Christian teaching.

While knowledge by itself may or may not be valuable, right knowledge or true doctrine is very important to God because it leads to godliness. This is confirmed throughout the New Testament, as in Titus 1:1 where Paul says that "the knowledge of the truth...leads to godliness." When the "being of light" that NDErs encounter asserts that he is not interested in doctrine he again reveals he is not the biblical God or the Lord Jesus Christ. Thus, what is not communicated by these experiences is the biblical truth that love for God and sound doctrine are inseparable (1 John 2:3-6; 5:3,9-12).

We can know that the NDE represents a spiritual deception because it leads people away from God's salvation and into a reliance on their own good works, which, coupled with the removal of the fear of death and the experience of the all-loving "being of light," makes them convinced that nothing else is needed to enter heaven at death.

## 8. Can NDEs precipitate the onset of psychic powers and contact with spirit guides?

In examining the correlation between the NDE and development of psychic abilities, we are establishing another connection to spiritistic influence, for psychic abilities are integrally connected with spiritism.[50]

Many researchers have noted that the NDE frequently leads to the development of psychic powers.[51] The research of Kenneth Ring, who includes an entire chapter on "NDEs and Psychic Development," leads one to conclude that the NDE can precipitate psychic powers and experiences as if the event itself had somehow opened the door to the psychic world—reminiscent of what occurs in occult initiations of all types. He observes, "I could not help noticing the frequency with which psychic events were spontaneously reported by NDErs and how often these experiences were said to have occurred following the NDE.... Many NDErs simply claimed that their psychic sensitivities have developed strikingly since their NDE."[52]

In fact, Ring views psychic development as a natural outgrowth of the NDE, as a part of the blossoming "fruit" from the implanted psychic seed: "Finally, as a byproduct of this spiritual development, NDErs tend to manifest a variety of psychic abilities afterward that are an inherent part of their transformation."[53] Ring also cites the research of psychiatrist Bruce Greyson, who "discovered that there was an increased incidence for virtually all of the psychic and psi-related phenomena he assessed,...."[54]

Richard Kohr is an educational researcher with the Pennsylvania Department of Education and a member of the research committee for the 40,000-member Association for Research and Enlightenment (founded by the famous medium Edgar Cayce), a group specializing in psychic practice and dissemination of occult material. Dr. Kohr also concludes that the NDE incident per se tends to lead to accelerated psychic development.[55] He remarks, "It is interesting to note that a variety of studies have revealed linkages among psi [psychic abilities], transcendent states, psi-related experiences, and NDEs."[56]

The all-loving, all-encompassing "Light" is the characteristic feature of the NDE.[57] As Dr. Morse says, "There are several ways to tap this spiritual energy. My guess is that the psychic powers to do so exist in all of us and that given the time and desire *we could see the Light* without having to die for it."[58] Indeed, through psychic development this happens all the time in the world of the occult.

With the onset of psychic abilities following the NDE, perhaps it is also not surprising that many people encounter personal spirit guides. For example, "Barbara stated that she has had more clairvoyant and telepathic experiences since her NDE.... She says that she is *much* more intuitive [i.e., psychic] than she was before and more in touch with an inner source of wisdom and has increased contact with spiritual guides."[59]

All in all, spiritistic encounters during and/or after the NDE appear to occur in a significant number of cases—in at least 20 percent and possibly up to 40 percent.[60]

But as we will see, the NDE can precipitate more than psychic experiences and encounters with spirits. It can also induce dramatic personality and worldview changes that undergird a permanent conversion to the occult.

## 9. Do NDEs frequently represent an initiation into the world of the occult?

Dr. Raymond Moody is the author of the smash bestseller *Life After Life.* For over 20 years, he has worked on the cutting edge of NDE research, talking with almost every NDE researcher in the world.[61] He is amazed at the tremendous power of the NDE: "The most impressive thing about NDEs to me is the enormous changes in personality that they bring about in people. That NDEs totally transform the people to whom they happen shows their reality and power."[62]

Unfortunately, for many people this NDE transformation is really part of a powerful initiation into the world of the occult. The presence of the "being of light" and the alleged dead, the development of psychic powers, the insulation against Christian belief, and the promotion of an occult philosophy and a liberal religious worldview prove this. While the NDE, in particular the deep NDE, tends to make people religious, even deeply religious, it does not make them Christian. In fact, it makes many people deeply religious in a way that is often anti-Christian. As we saw, it is true that distinct and usually positive personality changes may result. These changes, however, are often reminiscent of, though not always equivalent to, "higher self" transformations found in cultic, metaphysical, occult and New Age literature.[63]

For example, the NDErs' concept of God is more liberal, Eastern or occult (see Q. 11). From their initiation they *know* God loves and accepts them (and everyone else) apart from personal faith in Christ, and their basic, positive personality alteration tends to reinforce this conviction.[64] Thus, according to Ring, "The NDE not only changes an individual's life, but often completely and radically transforms it.... It would appear justified—again in some, surely not all, instances—to claim that NDEs tend to confer a new personal identity upon the NDEr as well as bring about major changes in behavior."[65]

Thus, the essence of the deep NDE is that it is a profoundly religious-occult experience that incorporates an often dramatic transformation of the individual. In the words of leading scientist and New Age proponent, Stanislav Grof, M.D., "The core NDE is a powerful catalyst of spiritual awakening and consciousness evolution. Its long term aftereffects include...[a] more open attitude toward reincarnation, and [the] development of [a] universal spirituality that transcends divisive interests of religious sectarianism and resembles the best of the mystical traditions or great Oriental philosophies."[66]

Ring himself observes, "The NDE is essentially a spiritual experience that serves as a catalyst for spiritual [i.e., occult] awakening and development."[67]

Consider again what the NDE frequently accomplishes. As a result of a brief encounter with "death," the participant experiences a dramatic religious "conversion type" personality change, an accompanying shift in worldview in harmony with the occult dynamics of the experience, a concern with alleged higher consciousness, the development of psychic powers, and the felt need to share the profound glories of the experience with others. Furthermore, the experience and its aftereffects appear to "grow" on the person, as if following the plan of some intelligent purpose.[68]

We cannot possibly list and evaluate all the published material relevant to categorizing the NDE as a potentially powerful occult initiation and transformation. Nevertheless, we may in very brief fashion note the following five points:

(a) *The NDE can be a consuming mystical experience:* Some researchers describe what NDErs encounter as "cosmic consciousness."[69] For example, psychologist Dr. John Pennachio, writing in "Near-Death Experience As Mystical Experience," observes the correlation of the NDE to Walter Pahnke's classic nine-point typology of mystical experience, noting that "such transformations are also characteristic of near-death experience.... A considerable number of near-death experiences move the subject toward attributes characteristic of mystical states. It is as if there is a brief, but intense program in mysticism.... Spiritual values, the higher self, and higher consciousness come to influence life."[70]

(b) *The NDE may resemble experiences induced by psychedelic drugs such as LSD and Hashish:* The extensive LSD research of psychiatrist Stanislav Grof reveals notable similarities between the NDE and experiences with LSD: "The experiences of patients under the influence of lysergic acid diethylamide (LSD) are remarkably similar to those described in the [Raymond] Moody model [of the composite NDE]...."[71]

In "Hashish Near-Death Experience" R.K. Siegel and A.E. Hirschman, of the Department of Psychiatry and Biobehavioral Sciences School of Medicine at UCLA, note that "intoxication with hallucinogens has been associated with numerous subjective reports of death and dying. From the magical-religious uses of plant hallucinogens by New World Indians, through the psychedelic-assisted therapy of terminally ill cancer patients, to the recreational ecstasies of New Age users, the literature is replete with reports of hallucinations containing elements of near-death experiences (NDEs).... Perhaps more than any other hallucinogen, hashish has been associated with such NDEs."[72]

They then proceed to observe the parallels with spiritistic influence in both the NDE and hashish-induced NDEs.

(c) *The NDE can be related to yogic kundalini arousal:* Classical Hindu *kundalini* symptomatology (dramatic experiences with energy possession) has strong parallels with demon possession.[73] Thus, it is significant that Ring reports, "In full kundalini awakenings, what is experienced is significantly similar to what many NDErs report from their experiences. And more than that: the aftereffects of these deep kundalini awakenings seem to lead to individual transformations and personal worldviews *essentially indistinguishable* from those found in NDErs."[74]

Indeed, according to Ring, "it seems that kundalini arousal gives one access to the same (or a similar) dimension of consciousness as does the core NDE."[75] This is why some NDErs have reported their belief that NDEs actually "*activate* kundalini energy."[76]

The nature of the deep NDE makes it evident that it is not a unique experience, but rather it is simply one of many forms of occult initiation—as other researchers have recognized.[77] This would explain the development of psychic powers as well as other aftereffects that are natural components of occult initiation and demonic energizing. Even Ring confesses that what happens during the NDE "has nothing inherently to do with death or with the transition to death...[and that] this point cannot be emphasized too strongly...."[78]

He cites psychiatrist Stanley Dean's ten-point typology of "ultra-consciousness" and its similarity to the NDE, showing that the NDE is merely part of a larger worldwide trend involving the development of occult consciousness.[79] In other words, the NDE can involve full-blown occult transformation. The fact that it happens to occur in conjunction with a brush with death does not change this fact. What apparently is unique, however, is that some people are having this experience *without seeking it.*

(d) *The deep NDE involves a powerful transforming energy—an occult regeneration:* As further evidence of occult transformation in the NDE, we should observe that the person having a deep NDE is evidently infused with occult energy—and that for some this condition appears to be permanent: According to Ring, "The implication is that qualities of the light somehow infuse themselves into the *core* of the experiencer's being so as to lead to a *complete union* with the light. . . . the testimony from more than one core experiencer indicates that there is a *direct transmission of the light's energy into themselves* and that what is absorbed in that encounter with the light in that moment outside of time *remains with them* when they return to the world of time. In short, the seeds of transformation appear to be implanted during the NDE."[80]

Obviously, if mystical energies are transferred and directly absorbed by a person, and remain, it would not be altogether improbable that some kind of, for lack of a better word, spiritual "operation" or occult regeneration might have been performed. After all, look at the variety of dramatic changes that ensue.

It is significant that these people report that they *merge* or *fuse with* this "light" which they interpret as God. Biblically, of course, this is impossible, for the biblical God "alone possesses immortality and dwells in *unapproachable* light; whom no man has seen or can see" (1 Timothy 6:16, emphasis added). In other words, whatever the "light" is they are approaching and merging with, it is not the essence of God. Rather, this sounds like the old pagan initiations of the East and the occult, whose energy infusions are characteristically associated with *demonization*.[81] And if so, it is not surprising that for many people the NDE constitutes a *permanent* occult transformation.[82]

(e) *The NDE is relevant to occult and pagan religion, ancient and modern:* A number of studies have been done that reveal the importance of the NDE to the beliefs of various occult religions, including Mormonism, Swedenborgianism, and Tibetan Buddhism.[83]

The NDE also appears to be markedly similar to the transformations generated by the ancient pagan mystery religions. Ring comments on the essential agreement of the NDE and the ancient Egyptian Osirian rituals as to information learned: "Certainly no one familiar with the literature on the near-death experience could fail to notice the many parallels, both in phenomenology and after-effects, between the Egyptian initiation and the NDE. . . . The NDE is, in its essence, identical to what the Osirian candidate learned during his initiation."[84]

In other words, by a profound occult experience, the initiate comes to realize that death is an illusion and that his true self is immortal.[85] Thus, one purpose of the ancient rituals was to employ hypnosis, magic and occult forces to induce the spirit to leave the body in experiential "confirmation" of occult truth about the illusion of death. The initiate was taught this lesson in the most profound way possible—by being made to experience within himself the process of dying and entering another dimension.

All of this is why so many people who have NDEs become enamored with the world of the occult. Indeed, we have talked with a number of individuals who became professional occultists (astrologers, Tarot readers, etc.) as a result of their NDE—and not infrequently as a result of their obedience to the commands of the spirits they met during their NDE.

But this new interest in occultism also occupies many who were only initially interested in researching the field of NDE phenomena. Dr. Elisabeth Kubler-Ross, a leading thanatologist, now has spirit guides, does astral travel and believes in reincarnation from her "past lives" experience.[86] Dr. Raymond Moody also decided to "look more closely" at occult writings after his initial research.[87] And, as we saw, parapsychologist Dr. Karlis Osis found great confirmation of the occult, mediumistic worldview after his NDE research. Liberal minister Archie Matson now advocates mediumism and occult practices,[88] and psychic Harold Sherman now supports necromancy via meditation.[89]

In conclusion, the above data prove that the near-death experience is, for many people, a dramatic conversion to the consequential world of the occult.[90] When Ring confesses that "what occurs during the NDE has nothing inherently to do with death or the transition to death,"[91] he is entirely correct.

## 10. What about reincarnation experiences and the NDE?

In their own unique way, NDEs may lead to an openness towards the pagan doctrine of reincarnation and sympathy toward Eastern religions in general.[92] Ring comments that "NDErs do appear to be more inclined to a reincarnational perspective following their experience and, not surprisingly, appear to be more sympathetic to Eastern religions as well. Furthermore, my findings seem to be consistent with the data of other researchers."[93] For example, the characteristic "review" of one's life is sometimes transformed into a review of one's alleged *past* lives.[94] This NDE association with reincarnation is also one more parallel to ancient mystery religion. Of course, mediumism and spirit guides in general tend to encourage a belief in reincarnation, which is a common occult philosophy. But along with many other researchers we are convinced that the most logical explanation for reincarnation experiences can be found in demonic deception, not in the existence of multiple lifetimes.[95]

## 11. What is the NDE view of God?

The NDE generates a firm conviction concerning the existence of God. But, whatever else it may be, the "God" experienced by NDErs is not the biblical God. Many NDErs think they have encountered the biblical God or Jesus. Unfortunately, this appears to be a misperception based on people's spiritual expectations from a nominal exposure to Christian belief.

First, this God is not necessarily personal. The NDE God is described in terms such as the following: "An undeniable omnipresent *force*." "It is *not* a person, but it is a being of some kind. It is a massive energy."[96]

Second, this God seems to be indifferent to evil. For example, one NDEr relates, "I remember I knew that everything, everywhere in the universe was okay, that the plan was perfect. That whatever was happening—the wars, famine, whatever—was okay. Everything was perfect. Somehow it was all a part of the perfection, that we didn't have to be concerned about it at all."[97] This, too, is in harmony with the philosophy of the East and the occult.

Third, God may also be perceived in pantheistic terms so that "God is all, all is God." Another NDEr's comment typifies this: "I seem to have greater awareness of all living things and that we are all a part of one another and ultimately a part of a greater consciousness, God."[98] A former atheist concludes that now, "I know that there is a God. And that God is everything that exists, [that's] the essence of God.... Everything that exists has the essence of God within it. I *know* there's a God now. I have no question."[99] And, "I think of God as a tremendous source of energy.... We are [all] God."[100]

Finally, after the NDE, God is often seen as the originator of all religions, and NDErs may find they desire a universal religion that embraces all humanity.[101] The conclusion is: "No matter what religion you are in, of the five major religions...you are still worshiping the one God, no matter what you call it: Allah, God, Jesus, or whoever."[102]

All this reveals that the "God" that many NDErs encounter is not the biblical God.[103]

## 12. Are all NDEs positive experiences—or are many hellish?

All NDEs are not positive. But researchers such as Raymond Moody, Elisabeth Kubler-Ross, Kenneth Ring and others—who often accept an occult view of life and death—seem to rarely encounter people with negative experiences. According to Dr. Moody, far fewer than 1 percent of people experience hellish NDEs (.3 percent). This figure is based on several thousand NDEs involving the research of Drs. Moody, and Ring, and the Evergreen Study.[104] Therefore, these researchers would have us think that, for almost everyone, life after death is entirely a heavenly affair.

Nevertheless, other researchers report some far different NDEs from those that entail universal bliss. One leading researcher, Dr. Charles Garfield, recalls, "Not everyone dies a blissful, accepting death.... Almost as many of the dying patients I interviewed reported negative visions (encounters with demonic figures and so forth) as reported blissful experiences, while some reported both."[105]

Hellish experiences are also reported by Dr. Maurice Rawlings M.D., in *Beyond Death's Door* (1978), and in *Is It Safe to Die?* (in press). Rawlings also suggests that positive and negative experiences occur in a roughly 50–50 ratio. He discovered that the positive experiences are easily remembered because they are so blissful. But the negative experiences are so hellish they are repressed deeply enough so that they are not remembered at all.

We should remind the reader that, as in the case of occult astral projection or soul travel, the NDE appears to be nothing more than an experience wherein one is temporarily suspended outside the body in another dimension. It is not an experience with true or irreversible death. So, it is not an experience of death as defined biblically—it is neither heaven nor hell. Thus, we do not believe that the vast majority of cases can properly be described as experiences of the biblical afterlife. In other words, it is a mistake to interpret these experiences as "visits" to either heaven or hell. They are mystical experiences that the spirits would like us to think are accurate representations of heaven or hell. Thus, the NDE "heaven" is accessible to anyone irrespective of his religious belief, and the NDE "hell"—as in cross-cultural traditions—is at best only a temporary place for the purging of sins and is not eternal. However, in neither case is the depiction true to biblical teaching. (Although this is not to say there are no cases where the biblical heaven or hell might have been experienced.)

In conclusion, the bias of some NDE researchers not withstanding,[106] we stress the importance of a critical approach to NDEs. We should not be so gullible as to accept the claim that all NDEs are blissful. Likewise, neither should we assume that such experiences—whether heavenly or hellish—are accurate descriptions of the biblical afterlife.

## 13. What are some additional implications of the NDE?

By now, tens of millions of people have been exposed to the "death is glorious" theme in one way or another. But in the last ten years there have also been reports in the media of suicides apparently induced by the desire to experience the "glorious" nature of death as commonly reported in NDE literature.

This phenomenon also has its parallel in the occult. In the world of mediumism, spiritism, Eastern religion, and other forms of the occult, one not infrequently finds that those who seek out the spirits may become their victims through occult-induced mental illness and even through suicide. In fact, the spirits may cunningly counsel their contacts to commit suicide in order that they might experience "enlightenment" sooner or be reunited with their "loved ones."[107]

In some cases, an inducement to suicide may also result from the NDE. While those with partial NDEs usually express gratitude at being brought back to life, others with more powerful experiences may resent it deeply and become depressed or even wish to die: Says one NDEr, "I just kept withdrawing more and more into my own world. I really didn't have much desire to go on living. I really wanted to go back to the tunnel....I really wanted to die."[108] And another admits, "The most depressed, the most severe anxiety I've ever had was at the moment I realized I must return to this earth. That is the greatest depths of depression I personally have ever had since that time or before."[109]

One can only wonder. With millions of people already suffering from depression in our country, will the knowledge that "death is bliss" provide a welcome relief and help justify their final act? Is it only coincidental that an increasing social acceptance of suicide coincides with the widespread reporting of blissful NDEs?

Some claim that NDEs will not lead to an increase in suicide because suicide-related NDEs are allegedly so unpleasant. But studies of suicide-induced NDEs reveal that these experiences are very similar to non-suicide-related NDEs. "The data offered no support to the claims of some researchers that suicide-induced NDEs are unpleasant."[110]

It is impossible to gauge how many suicides may eventually result from the widespread exposure to the positive NDE report. But there may be other consequences as well. Hundreds of NDErs apparently feel they have been "led" into counseling ministries with the terminally ill for the express purpose of conveying the "truth" about death.[111] In fact, many who research NDEs believe that nurses and other health professionals should specifically be trained to impart the NDE view of death to those who are dying. Of course, whether this is something good depends on the nature of death. Is it really an omnipresent bliss for everyone, including the unrepentant? Or does the biblical portrait of an eternal hell, confirmed by Jesus, describe the real nature of death for those not saved?

Finally, NDEs may also precipitate depression, divorce and other problems, including alienation from ordinary reality.[112] For example, it has been noted that "primary relationships are often subject to great strain following an NDE, and a considerable number of NDErs end up by divorcing their spouses, or at least wanting to."[113]

In conclusion, whether or not the NDE itself is heavenly its end results may not be.

## 14. What about children who have NDEs?

When discussing this issue, we need to remember two things: (1) that God protects children because they are special to Him (Psalm 127:3), and (2) that such protection may, in some circumstances, be thwarted or rejected by the child himself, depending on his age and circumstances. Biblically, we know that Jesus taught that the kingdom of God belonged to children and that children (at least) have guardian angels (Matthew 19:14; 18:10). However, the Bible also records at least one case of a demonized child and occult literature has many others.[114]

Children who are exposed to the occult may be influenced or harmed by it. For example, parents who train their children to accept occult practices harm them spiritually.[115] Regrettably, as our culture increasingly accepts the occult, children are increasingly exposed to it. Thankfully, many and perhaps most childhood NDEs do not seem to be occult. But some are.

Not surprisingly, children do not have the characteristic review of one's life, but some do experience the tunnel, the "being of light," dead relatives and other components of the adult NDE. Unfortunately, even the small amount of research done to date indicates that these experiences frequently become the basis for these children accepting false views about God and death as adults. For example, Melvin Morse, M.D. has written the runaway bestseller *Closer to the Light: Learning From the Near-Death Experiences of Children*. It is based on conversations with hundreds of his patients, including children who had NDEs and adults who remembered NDEs as children.

In discussing his research with childhood NDEs, Dr. Morse comments that "the near-death experiences of children remind us of forgotten ancient truths." And he gives examples of similar NDEs in ancient pagan religion such as the Egyptian mystery religion of Osiris, *The Egyptian Book of the Dead*, and *The Tibetan Book of the Dead*.[116]

In other words, even the childhood NDE can present us with a false message of universalism—that all will be saved, and that God is primarily concerned with good deeds, not specific religious belief. These childhood experiences can open the doors to a variety of occult pursuits later on in adulthood such as spiritism, developing psychic powers, and uniting medicine and the occult.[117]

For example, children who experience supposedly benevolent and loving spirit entities that act as their "guides" during an NDE may be more open to the general claims of spiritism later in life, such as in channeling. Without a biblical corrective to guard against spiritual deception, such NDEs might predispose a person toward accepting the occult. The issue then becomes whether or not children are protected by a proper interpretation of their experience. Consider some examples catalogued by Melvin Morse, M.D., in his book on near-death experiences of children.

A seven-year-old girl, raised as a Mormon, had an NDE where she saw two young boys who were "souls waiting to be born"—as well as her late grandfather and other dead people. This NDE supported Mormon doctrine relating to the dead (necromancy) as well as to preexistence (of souls waiting to be born to their life on earth). One teenager who had an NDE realized "that death was not to be feared" and that "the only real fear is not accomplishing our work in this life." One child met a "guardian angel" during her NDE which has remained with her throughout her adult life as her spiritual "guide." A nine-year-old girl's NDE resulted in her religious life being guided by that experience. Today, at 43, she "believes only in a vague conception of God" and is convinced that "being one with God is something that can be done without rules." A 50-year-old man who had his NDE at nine comments: "I know that where we are going is a beautiful place," and "because of that [NDE] I have never carried that burden of fear with me that many people have about death." A 33-year-old housewife who had her NDE at seven continues to have out-of-body experiences in her adult life. A five-year-old boy's NDE left him with two strong convictions. First, that life is precious and that death should not be feared. Second, that everyone is born with the knowledge he needs to solve life's problems and that "the answers are all inside" a person. A 54-year-old woman believes that her NDE at 15 years old has made her more tolerant of other people's beliefs and has given her a belief in reincarnation—but *not* a belief in God.[118]

Dr. Moody notes, "When individuals have an NDE at a very early age, it seems to get incorporated into their personality. It is something they live with all their lives, and it changes them."[119]

Whether it occurs in childhood or adulthood, the NDE may encourage individuals to become better people and give them meaning to life and devotion to humanity. But again, it does not appear to lead them to salvation in Christ: instead, it frequently inhibits it. For example, children who have NDEs seem to become model teenagers,[120] but they also have no fear of death and think that God is with them entirely apart from a personal faith in Christ. The "God" they experience is never identified. It seems that all they are left with is an uncertain understanding of who or what God is. Thus, children who have NDEs are not brought into a personal saving knowledge of God and Christ (John 17:3), but have only a powerful understanding that some nebulous God exists.

Further, the specific messages given to the children involve the basic teaching of a "social gospel": that being good and having a social conscience is the principal means of doing God's will.[121] Thus, "The message from the Light is almost always one that encourages [the gaining of] knowledge" [i.e., gnosticism], and the messages given to these children of the Light are not new or controversial. They are as old as mankind itself and have served as the primary fuel of our great religions: "Be the best that you can be." "Contribute to society." "Be nice, kind, and loving."[122]

# SECTION TWO

## The
## Cultic View
## of Death

### 15. What is the cultic view of death?

We use the term "cultic" descriptively, rather than pejoratively, to refer to those groups that claim a large degree of allegiance to the Bible and yet simultaneously deny its basic teachings. Also, there may be considerable overlap between the cults' teachings on death and the occult philosophy of death.

In general, when we describe the cultic view of death, we are referring specifically to three unbiblical but often related teachings concerning death and the afterlife: (1) Universalism assumes that all men have immortal souls and all will be saved. (2) Annihilationism assumes the immortality of the soul, but teaches that God will forever annihilate all who are not saved—their immortality will be taken from them at judgment. (3) Conditional immortality assumes the soul of man is not immortal, and therefore those not saved are simply never resurrected to eternal life. Nothing is taken from them or added to them; they merely cease to exist.[123]

None of these views are biblical, and yet they are not only characteristic teachings in the world of the cults and to some degree the occult, but they are also increasingly found in the Church as well. What these views have in common is their denial of the biblical teaching on an eternal hell. Like NDErs, people who accept these doctrines have no fear of eternal punishment after death.

### 16. What are some contemporary examples of the cultic view of death?

The citations below come from both cultic and occult literature. At least half originate directly in revelations from the spirit world.

*Christian Science*, founded by spiritist Mary Baker Eddy,[124] teaches that "there is no death"[125] because after death we

33

"awake only to another sphere of experience, and must pass through another probationary state...."[126] Thus, to Christian Scientists "heaven and hell are states of thought, not places. People experience their own heaven or hell right here...."[127]

*Edgar Cayce*, a spiritist and New Age prophet, says that "the destiny of the soul, as of all creation, is to become One with the Creator" and that no soul is ever lost.[128]

New Age cult leader and spiritist Sun Myung Moon, of *The Unification Church*, believes that "God will not desert any person eternally. By some means...they will be restored."[129]

*Mormonism*, founded by occultist Joseph Smith, argues, "The false doctrine that the punishment to be visited upon erring souls is endless...is but a dogma of unauthorized and erring sectaries, at once unscriptural, unreasonable, and revolting...."[130]

*The Worldwide Church of God* (Armstrongism), founded by Herbert W. and Garner Ted Armstrong, also asserts that hell is a false belief: "This final punishment which sinners suffer is eternal DEATH by fire.... Once they are burned up and now dead they are going to stay dead forever.... Those who teach the pagan doctrine of the immortality of the soul...teach contrary to what Jesus said!"[131]

*Jehovah's Witnesses*, founded by Charles Taze Russell, maintains that the wicked are forever annihilated because "The teaching about a fiery hell...can rightly be designated as a 'teaching of demons.'"[132]

*The Church of the New Jerusalem* (Swedenborgianism), founded by the spiritist Emanuel Swedenborg, emphasizes that God "does not condemn anyone to hell...."[133]

*Eckankar*, a New Age religion founded by Paul Twitchell and Darwin Gross, insists that "there is no death..."[134] and that there is no eternal hell.[135]

*Unity School of Christianity*, founded by occult dabblers Charles and Myrtle Fillmore, maintains: "There is no warrant for the belief that God sends man to everlasting punishment."[136]

*The Church Universal and Triumphant*, founded by New Age occultists Mark and Elizabeth Prophet, declares that Christian ministers are all false prophets and "wolves in sheep's clothing [who] preach from the pulpits of the world They have...spawned a luciferian theology and through their sorcery have exercised a hypnotic control over the people, . . . through their satanic lies of hellfire and damnation."[137]

*Christadelphianism*, founded by Dr. John Thomas, contends: "Those not worthy of resurrection to eternal life will find their destiny in the eternal oblivion of the grave."[138] And, "It follows also, of necessity, that the popular theory of hell and 'eternal torments' is a fiction."[139]

*Lucis Trust* and The Arcane School/Full Moon Meditation Groups, begun by New Age spiritist Alice Bailey, argue that "the fear of death is based upon . . . old erroneous teaching as to heaven and hell. . . ."[140]

*The Love Family* (The Children of God), founded by spiritist David Berg, views hell as a temporal purgatory: "the lake of fire is where the wicked go to get purged from their sins. . . . to let them eventually come . . . out."[141]

*Divine Science*, founded by the Brooks Sisters, maintains that "the 'lake of fire' is not hell as a place, but is God's consuming love in which our false beliefs about devil, death and hell are utterly destroyed." And thus, "Even death is a form of healing."[142]

*Rosicrucianism*, an occult philosophy, declares that "the 'eternal damnation' of those who are not 'saved' does not mean destruction nor endless torture, . . ."[143] and that "the Christian religion did not originally contain any dogmas about Hell. . . ."[144]

*Unitarian Universalism* confesses the following: "It seems safe to say that no Unitarian Universalist believes in a resurrection of the body, a literal heaven or hell, or any kind of eternal punishment. . . ."[145]

*The Mighty I Am*, founded by occultist Guy Ballard (Godfre Ray King), claims that "there is no death."[146] Rather, "Human beings are the only creators of 'hell.' . . . Each individual carries his own heaven or hell with him . . . for these are but the results of mental and emotional states."[147]

*The Theosophical Society*, founded by medium Helena P. Blavatsky, declares: "we positively refuse to accept the . . . belief in eternal reward or eternal punishment. . . ."[148] Hence, "Death . . . is not . . . a cause for fear."[149]

The spirits everywhere proclaim their allegiance to this cultic teaching. "Ramtha," the spirit speaking through medium J.Z. Knight, claims: "God has never judged you or anyone" and, "No, there is no Hell and there is no devil."[150] "Lilly" and other spirits channeled through medium Ruth

Montgomery argue that "there is no such thing as death" and that "God punishes no man."[151]

In conclusion, the cultic view of death has much in common with the NDE, including (1) occult origins, (2) its emphasis that hell is a false teaching, and (3) that death, far from something to be feared, merely opens the door to other levels of spiritual progression.

### 17. Is the Christian Church increasingly abandoning the teaching of Jesus and adopting a cultic view of death?

Today, what was once relegated to cultic belief is now openly taught as part of "Christian" teaching.[152] Despite the Bible's mentioning hell some 50 times, opinion polls reveal that 70 percent of all clergy deny the doctrine of hell.[153] Some highly respected evangelical scholars and educated laymen have also rejected the doctrine of hell. They teach that conditional immortality, annihilationism or universalism are legitimate options for Christian belief. Unfortunately, they are influencing others to conclude that life is far safer than what Jesus and the Church have traditionally taught.

When a conditionalist text such as *The Fire That Consumes* is chosen as an alternate selection by the Evangelical Book Club and when, as some have claimed, "Over 50 percent of young evangelicals believe" in universalism and reject the doctrine of hell, we have to wonder.[154]

Dr. J.I. Packer has noted that universalism "has in this century quietly become part of the orthodoxy of many Christian thinkers and groups."[155] Likewise, D.B. Eller asserts in the *Evangelical Dictionary of Theology* that it is clear that "Universalism, in a variety of forms, continues to have appeal for contemporary faith, in both liberal and conservative circles."[156] Theologian Steven Travis observes, "In recent years very few theologians have expounded and defended [the] traditional approach" of eternal hell.[157]

As Dr. Vernon Grounds once commented, "Seldom, I suppose, do we find ourselves brooding over the awesome doctrine of eternal punishment. Only on rarest occasions and then fleetingly is our mood that of Rodin's famous statue, 'The Thinker,' who sits in mute amazement watching lost souls enter hell. What William Gladstone wrote about eternal punishment in the late 19th century is equally true today: it 'seems to be relegated at present to the far off corners of the Christian mind, and there to sleep in deep shadow.'"[158]

Richard J. Bauckham, lecturer in the history of Christian thought at the University of Manchester, also points out the neglect of this doctrine when he writes, "Until the nineteenth century almost all Christian theologians taught the reality of eternal torment in hell ... [for them it was] as indispensable a part of universal Christian belief as the doctrines of the Trinity and the Incarnation. Since 1800 this situation has entirely changed, and no traditional doctrine has been so widely abandoned as that of eternal punishment. Its advocates among theologians today must be fewer than ever before.... Among the less conservative, universal salvation, either as hope or as dogma, is now so widely accepted that many theologians assume it virtually without argument."[159]

In some ways this abandonment of traditional doctrine is not unexpected. In the following sobering words, the Holy Spirit explicitly warns, "The Spirit clearly says that in later times some will abandon the faith and follow deceiving spirits and things taught by demons" (1 Timothy 4:1 NIV). When Christians reject the doctrine of hell, perhaps they have forgotten with whom they are siding.

We have proven that the rejection of eternal punishment is the common teaching of not just the cults, the occult and the New Age Movement but specifically of the spirit world as well. For example, the famous Arthur Conan Doyle, author of the Sherlock Holmes series, became converted to mediumism and spiritism. In his book *The New Revelation* he observes, "All spirit people (spirits) of wisdom know that there is no burning hell, no fearful devil."[160] So, the conclusion would seem unavoidable. When Christians adopt the same teaching on hell as given by demons through their human hosts—as in channeling and other forms of mediumism—they are, in effect, "paying attention to the doctrines of demons."

Is the Church willing to accept such a deplorable state of affairs—when it offers to its own people the teachings of the cults and demons? In rejecting hell, is the Church listening more to the devil than to its own Lord?

The truth is that hell is a vital Christian doctrine. As Vernon Grounds observes, "It is impossible to exaggerate the seriousness and urgency that the doctrine of hell imparts to life here and now."[161] It should not be abandoned. It should be preached from the pulpits, in Bible schools and seminaries, within and without the Church.

# SECTION THREE

## *The Biblical View of Death: Eternal Heaven or Hell*

### 18. What is the biblical view of death?

Death per se is a condition of *separation*. According to the Bible, there are only two kinds of death. First, there is physical death, which involves the *temporary* separation of the spirit from the body. In the resurrection, the body is later rejoined with the human spirit. Second, there is spiritual death or the *eternal* separation of the human spirit from God. This condition has no remedy.

Death is not good—it has never been good. Physical death—separation from the body—is not good since man is left "unclothed" (2 Corinthians 5:4; Philippians 3:21; 1 Corinthians 15) and in an unnatural state. Spiritual death—separation from God—is also obviously not good since it is eternal.

"Death" and "life" are irreconcilable and opposite *conditions of existence* in both this life and the next. Apart from Christ, death leads to one thing only—eternal judgment ("It is given for man to die once and then comes judgment" Hebrews 9:27). But *with* Christ, death leads to life: "I am the resurrection and the life; he who believes in Me shall live even if he dies, and everyone who lives and believes in Me shall never die" (John 11:25-26). And, "Truly, truly, I say to you, he who hears My word, and believes Him who sent Me, has eternal life, and does not come into judgment, but has passed out of death into life" (John 5:24).

The Bible teaches that prior to salvation, even as they are alive, all men and women exist in a state of spiritual death or separation from God. Their human spirits are dead to those things that God is truly concerned about (see Luke 15:24-32; Ephesians 2:1; 1 Timothy 5:6; Revelation 3:1). Even though they are alive physically, they do not consider the one true God, nor do they thank Him, nor do they care about His interests. Whatever concept of God they may believe in, they do not accept the one true God. This is why

Jesus Himself referred to "the dead burying their own dead," explicitly teaching that the living human beings around him were, as far as God was concerned, spiritually dead (Luke 9:60; Romans 3:10-18).

The Bible tells us that physical and spiritual death exist for one reason—sin. God warned Adam and Eve that if they disobeyed Him, in that day, they would die (Genesis 2:17). This is why the Bible teaches that "the wages of sin is death" (Romans 6:23).

Because sin causes death, the problem of sin must be dealt with before death can be eradicated. This is the reason for the Christian teaching on the Atonement—that Christ died for the sins of the world. As Jesus taught, "For God so loved the world that he gave his only begotten Son that whoever believes in him should not perish but have eternal life" (John 3:16). Whoever receives Christ as his personal Savior is "born again" or made alive spiritually. That person receives true life after death or, in biblical terms, eternal life (John 6:47). But what actually happens, of course, is that the believer's state of spiritual death is cancelled at the point of receiving Christ. There is no longer the possibility of suffering God's judgment for his sins, which is the second death. Instead, at the point of physical death, he will join God forever. This is the essence of the term "saved." But it must be stressed that the system is conditional. Men must believe in the atoning death of Jesus Christ or they cannot be saved. This is the condition: that they accept what God has done in the person of Christ.

The Christian hope then is in physical resurrection and eternal immortality based on Christ's resurrection and life, not a mediumistic view of gradual, spiritual self-progression after death (Romans 4:25; 1 Corinthians 6:14; 2 Corinthians 4:14; 5:1; Ephesians 1:15-21; 2:4-10; Philippians 1:21; 3:21; Colossians 3:4, etc.). Those who accept Christ inherit heaven for eternity, while those who reject God's mercy inherit hell for eternity.

Thus, the biblical view is that the saved are with God— they go to be with Him at the moment of death (Luke 23:43; John 12:26; Acts 7:59; 2 Corinthians 5:8; Philippians 1:23, etc.) while the unsaved dead are confined and under punishment. Furthermore, there is no possibility of altering one's condition after death. Death, then, is not extinction, as many cults teach. It does not involve a condition of reincarnation, where the soul experiences many lifetimes, as the occult believes. It does not involve a condition of ultimate union or absorption into some impersonal, divine essence, as many Eastern religions teach (Ecclesiastes 12:5; Luke

12:46-47; 16:19-31; Acts 1:25; Hebrews 9:27; Psalms 78:39; 2 Corinthians 5:11; Hebrews 10:31; 12:27-29; 2 Peter 2:4,9; Revelation 20:10,15).

Of course, if the saved are with Christ and the unsaved are confined and in judgment, then the dead are not free to roam around, and therefore not who they claim to be. This takes us to our next question.

### 19. What is the biblical view of the afterlife?

What about the NDE and the Bible? The biblical view of death is far different from that which is implied by the NDE, but this is not to say that the NDE is necessarily unreal or imaginary. The spirit does, in fact, leave the body at true death (Luke 8:55; 1 Kings 17:22; Ecclesiastes 12:6-7). It is at least theoretically possible that some natural "trigger mechanism" or spiritistic influence could occasionally produce a similar result prior to death. It may be possible, then, to temporarily enter a spiritual dimension where, for example, angels (both good and evil) might exist.

In occult literature spirits have claimed the ability to induce out-of-body experiences in humans.[162] And biblically we are told that the devil does have, in some sense, an influence over death (Hebrews 2:14). In our opinion, the evidence from the testimony of psychics, gurus, occultists, etc. regarding astral projection or out-of-body experiences indicates that the separation of the body and spirit of the living is a temporarily possible condition. Exactly where they go in something like astral travel is unknown. But one also cannot rule out demonic deception, or a manipulation of the mind that only gives people the feeling of being out of their bodies when, in fact, they are not.[163]

Regardless, the NDE still does not supply a fully accurate description of the biblical heaven. The Bible describes heaven as an entirely new order of existence that is wonderful beyond comparison. But it is only for the redeemed. The common cultural myths—heaven as a reward for good deeds, people floating on clouds, plucking harps or polishing halos, Peter at the pearly gates checking invitations, etc.—are absent. What we can imagine from the biblical descriptions given is that the redeemed become spiritual in nature, changed completely. They become truly one with God, yet retain their unique individuality—spiritual beings who are distinct personalities and are not, as in Eastern traditions, absorbed into God. We are still who we are, but wonderfully recreated. The common analogy suggested from nature is that of the simple larva emerging as a magnificent butterfly.

Because the Scripture clearly teaches that God is love, a fact so thoroughly demonstrated at the cross, heaven will be a place that is imbued with love. It will be a completely loving environment—a place where we eternally enjoy the presence of the very essence of love, peace, joy, beauty, creativity, and everything that is sublime. This glorious future is hinted at in 1 Corinthians 2:9: "Things which eye has not seen and ear has not heard, and which have not entered the heart of man, all that God has prepared for those who love Him."

It is God's nature to give, and we can only guess at what God will give those He loves throughout eternity. Jesus simply said, "Great is our reward in heaven," and the Apostle Paul, who was surrounded with sufferings, assured us that "the sufferings of this present time are not even worthy to be compared with the glory that is to be revealed to us" (Romans 8:18).

Perhaps the most awesome fact of heaven is not only that we will be in the presence of Jesus, but also that we shall be "like Him" (1 John 3:2). We are reminded of the statement by C.S. Lewis that if any person on earth could now see one of the redeemed, they would be tempted to worship them as a god. Each of us shall be completely sinless, joyful, and powerful. We will not only know the personalities of the Bible, but also our own saved friends and relatives who have joined us for eternity, and even our "guardian angels" as we think of them. We will be content, with no wants. We will be with, talk with, and constantly commune with the God who loves us and has redeemed us forever. Time and space will no longer exist as we know them, but we will continue in fellowship with the Maker of time and space.

We will have every question answered, and yet because God is infinite there will be throughout eternity new things to learn about Him. But whatever we learn, we shall forever be mindful of the infinite love of God for us expressed in the life, death, and resurrection of His Son, Jesus Christ.

In essence, to inherit heaven is to inherit all that God is (1 Corinthians 3:21-23) and all that exists in His universe as He originally intended it.

But the Bible also teaches that there is an eternal hell for those who have willfully refused the love and mercy of God. In large measure, the real hell about hell is that people choose it for themselves. Theologian Harold O.J. Brown once commented that "Hell has been called 'the most enduring monument to the freedom of the human will.'"[164] C.S. Lewis emphasized, "There are only two kinds of people in the end: those who say to God, 'Thy will be done,' and those to whom God says, in the end, '*Thy* will be done.'"[165]

In his book *The Problem of Pain* Lewis expanded on this idea: "If a game is played, it must be possible to lose it. If the happiness of a creature lies in self-surrender, no one can make that surrender but himself (though many can help him to make it) and he may refuse. I would pay any price to be able to say truthfully 'all will be saved.' But my reason retorts, 'without their will, or with it?' If I say, 'without their will,' I at once perceive a contradiction; how can the supreme voluntary act of self-surrender be involuntary? If I say 'with their will,' my reason replies 'how if they *will not* give in?'"[166]

There is no other authority than the Bible when it comes to the subject of life after death. Occult experiences that are demonic deceptions cannot tell us about the afterlife, nor can cultic theology, nor endless human speculation from the dawn of time. Only God knows what death is like. And He has told us. Unfortunately, many people who swear by the passages on heaven in the Bible completely reject the passages on hell, however irrational this might be. We stress that God is "not wishing for any to perish, but for all to come to repentance. He desires all men to be saved and to come to the knowledge of the truth" (2 Peter 3:9; 1 Timothy 2:4). Nevertheless, for those who refuse to do so there is a place of punishment for their sins that is eternal.

Hell is described in the Bible in a variety of terms: "outer darkness," "the resurrection of judgment," "the black darkness," "the punishment of eternal fire," "the place where there is weeping and gnashing of teeth," "eternal punishment," etc. (Matthew 3:7-12; 8:12; 22:13; 25:46; Mark 9:43,48; John 5:29; Revelation 19:20; 20:10-15, etc.).

But why must hell be eternal? First, because God is an infinite being. Sins committed against Him require the full magnitude of a divine punishment based upon *infinite* holiness. Who can deny that infinite holiness might justly require eternal punishment? Further, without the punishment of evil, there is no justice in eternity. But can eternal justice coexist with temporal punishment if no amount of limited punishment has absolute meaning when compared to the timelessness of eternity? In other words, if, in eternity, there is to be divine justice—punishment of evil corresponding to the offended sensibilities of infinite holiness—one would think it must last forever or, by comparison, be ultimately meaningless. To punish someone for a million years and then bring them into heaven for all eternity is, comparatively speaking, hardly any punishment at all.

Second, those who were never redeemed in this life will continue in the same spiritual condition they nurtured on earth. Their unredeemed personality will exist eternally. In their feelings, thoughts, and will they shall constantly be expressing the fruits of their sinful nature. In other words, they will continue to sin forever. But the punishment for eternal sinning can only be eternal punishment.

Whether or not we can adequately comprehend hell, the Bible clearly teaches it. Jesus Himself taught that the unrepentant "will go away into eternal punishment" (Matthew 25:46).

Alternate cultic views cannot be defended biblically.

Conditional immortality teaches that the human spirit is not innately immortal. But no Scripture anywhere proves this, and it goes against the implication of man being created in God's image, and, therefore, of having an eternal spirit. On the other hand, to say that the human spirit *is* immortal but that it will be annihilated in judgment rather than face eternal punishment is also lacking in biblical support.

Universalism, the teaching that all will be saved, is also contradicted in scores of Scriptures, some of which we have cited.

Those who advocate the above beliefs frequently appeal to (1) philosophical arguments (e.g., infinite love and eternal punishment are mutually contradictory); (2) humanistic arguments, none of which are convincing (e.g., men are too good to be damned); and (3) scriptural or exegetical arguments (e.g., that the specific Greek and Hebrew words for eternal really do not mean eternal).

But the biblical words for eternal do mean eternal, and the words for punishment do mean punishment.[167]

In fact, the Scriptures are as clear on the doctrine of eternal punishment as they are on justification by faith or the deity of Jesus Christ. It is only emotional appeal, humanistic thinking, contaminated philosophy or preexisting bias against hell that can make a "case" for these unbiblical options.

The scriptural teaching on eternal punishment is not obscure or uncertain; the very difficulty of the doctrine argues for its biblical clarity. Given the natural tendency to reject something so unpleasant as hell, only scriptural certainty could explain the Church's position of acceptance for 2,000 years.

The problem is that many people today, including some Christians, refuse to accept what the Scriptures and their Lord plainly teach. In 2,000 years, all exegetical arguments that have ever been put forth to reject the doctrine of eternal punishment have failed. Therefore, conditional immortality, annihilationism, and universalism are mere humanistic speculations, not biblical or theological truths—and certainly not legitimate options for Christians.

In an area where neither reason nor emotion is sufficient, to reject the clear scriptural teaching on life after death is to assume agnosticism. As Dr. Packer observes, "To fall victim to secular philosophy and ideology has been a characteristic Protestant vice for three centuries, and it is one from which evangelicals are by no means free."[168]

# Conclusion

If each of us will die one day, then the most important thing in life is to have assurance that death can be entered safely. Whether or not we fear dying, we need not fear death if our sins are forgiven through faith in Christ. Do you desire to know the living God? Are you willing to acknowledge your sin before Him and to receive His Son? If so, we recommend the following prayer:

Lord Jesus Christ, *I humbly acknowledge* that I have sinned in my thinking, speaking and acting, that I am guilty of deliberate wrongdoing, that my sins have separated me from Your Holy presence, and that I am helpless to commend myself to You.

*I firmly believe* that You died on the cross for my sins, bearing them in Your own body and suffering in my place the condemnation they deserved.

*I have thoughtfully counted the cost of following You.* I sincerely repent, turning away from my past sins. I am willing to surrender to You as my Lord and Master. Help me not to be ashamed of You.

*So now I come to You.* I believe that for a long time You have been patiently standing outside the door knocking. I now open the door. Come in, Lord Jesus, and be my Savior and my Lord forever. Amen.[169]

# Notes

1. Stanislav Grof and Joan Halifax, *The Human Encounter with Death* (New York: Dutton, 1977), 1.
2. Verlyn Klinkenborg, "At the Edge of Eternity," *Life* Magazine (March 1992): 66.
3. E.g., Raymond Moody, *Life After Life: The Investigation of a Phenomenon—Survival of Bodily Death* (Atlanta: Mockingbird, 1976), 98.
4. Moody, *Life After Life*, 24.
5. E.g., Kurt Koch, *Christian Counseling and Occultism* (Grand Rapids: Kregel, 1972), 37-192.
6. Raymond A. Moody, *The Light Beyond: New Explorations by the Author of Life After Life* (New York: Bantam, 1989), 7-20.
7. Melvin Morse, M.D., *Closer to the Light: Learning from the Near-Death Experiences of Children* (New York: Villard Books, 1990), 105; cf. Mark Woodhouse, "Five Arguments Regarding the Objectivity of NDEs," *Anabiosis*, Vol. 3, No. 1.
8. Based on personal conversations and the initial research of those studying Christian NDEs such as Dr. Nina Helene; cf. John Weldon and Zola Levitt, *Is There Life After Death?* (Dallas: Zola Levitt Ministries, 1990), Ch. 8.
9. "Religion in America: 50 Years: 1935–1985," *The Gallup Report*, No. 236 (May 1985), 53; *U.S. News and World Report* (March 25, 1991): 57.
10. *The Gallup Report*, 53; see also *Death Studies*, Vol. 9, No. 2: 95 and *Psychology Today* (January 1981): 65.
11. Andrew Greeley, "Mysticism Goes Mainstream," *American Health* (January/February 1987): passim.
12. John Ankerberg and John Weldon, *Cult Watch: What You Need to Know About Spiritual Deception* (Eugene, OR: Harvest House, 1991), 167.
13. *U.S. News and World Report* (March 25, 1991): 57.
14. Robert Monroe, *Journeys Out of the Body*, passim; the published studies by Dr. Robert Crookall; Herbert Greenhouse, *The Astral Journey* (New York: Avon, 1976).
15. Compare Kenneth Ring's *Heading Toward Omega: In Search of the Meaning of the Near-Death Experience* (New York: William Morrow, 1985) and the books of Robert Monroe, et al., cited above.
16. Ring, *Heading*, 19.
17. Moody, *The Light Beyond*, 198.
18. Ring, *Heading*, 31.
19. Ring, *Heading*, 27.
20. Hebrews 13:8; Matthew 24:35.
21. Moody, *Life After Life*, 45-53, 70; the other published works of Drs. Moody and Ring cited above; *Anabiosis*, various issues; cf. *The Journal of Near-Death Studies* and *Theta*, relevant articles.
22. See John Ankerberg and John Weldon, *The Facts on the Occult* (Eugene, OR: Harvest House, 1992) and *Can You Trust Your Doctor?* (Irving, TX: Word, 1991), 87-94.
23. Raphael Gasson, *The Challenging Counterfeit* (Plainfield, NJ: Logos, 1971); Victor Ernest, *I Talked with Spirits* (Wheaton, IL: Tyndale, 1971); Johanna Michaelsen, *The Beautiful Side of Evil* (Eugene, OR: Harvest House, 1982); Doreen Irvine, *Freed from Witchcraft* (Nashville: Nelson, 1973); Ben Alexander, *Out from Darkness* (Joplin, MO: College Press, 1986).
24. Ring, *Heading*, 224.
25. cf. Ring, *Heading*, Chs. 3–8; Moody, *The Light Beyond*, passim. See note 21.
26. John White, "What the Dying See," *Psychic* Magazine (September/October 1976): 40.
27. D. Scott Rogo, "Research on Deathbed Experiences," *Parapsychology Today* (January/February, 1978): 21.
28. Frederick Myers, *Human Personality and Its Survival of Bodily Death* (New York: Longmans, Green & Co., 1935), 7.
29. Emanuel Swedenborg, *Heaven and Its Wonders and Hell* (New York: Swedenborg Foundation, 1940), 447-448.
30. Arthur Ford, *The Life Beyond Death* (New York: G.P. Putnam & Sons, 1971), 144-146.
31. Ibid., 158.
32. Jane Roberts, *Seth: Dreams and Projections of Consciousness* (Walpole, NH: Stillpoint, 1986), 193, 350.
33. Kenneth Ring and C.J. Rosing, "The Omega Project," *Journal of UFO Studies*, New Series, Vol. 2 (1990): 71.
34. Moody, *Life After Life*, 70.
35. Ring, *Heading*, 62.
36. Moody, *The Light Beyond*, 38-39.
37. Ring, *Heading*, 265.
38. Ibid., 112-113.
39. Moody, *The Light Beyond*, 27, 33-34.
40. Ibid., 41.
41. Ring, *Heading*, 265.

42. John J. Heaney, "Recent Studies of Near-Death Experiences," *Journal of Religion and Health*, Vol. 22, No. 2 (Summer 1983): 127.
43. E.g., Malachi Martin, *Hostage to the Devil* (New York: Bantam, 1977), 132-135. See note 62.
44. Moody, *The Light Beyond*, 49.
45. Ibid.
46. Ibid., 88.
47. Ibid., 39.
48. Ibid., 87-88.
49. Ibid., 162-163.
50. Ankerberg and Weldon, *Cult Watch*, 257-260, 268-270.
51. Cf. Bruce Greyson, "Increase in Psychic and Psi-Related Phenomena Following Near-Death Experiences," *Theta* (in press); Richard Kohr, "Near-Death Experience and Its Relationship to Psi and Various Altered States," *Theta*, Vol. 10 (1982): 50-53; Kenneth Ring, "Paranormal and Other Non-Ordinary Aspects of Near-Death Experiences," *Essence*, Vol. 5 (1981): 33-51; Kenneth Ring, "Precognitive and Prophetic Visions in Near-Death Experiences," *Anabiosis*, Vol. 2 (1982): 47-74 and more recent studies.
52. Ring, *Heading*, 166-174.
53. Ibid., 166.
54. Ibid., 180.
55. Richard Kohr, "Near-Death Experiences, Altered States, Psi- Sensitivity," *Anabiosis*, Vol. 3, No. 2 (Dec. 1983): 152.
56. Ibid.
57. Morse, *Closer*, 115-116.
58. Ibid., 126.
59. Ring, *Heading*, 172-173.
60. Moody, *The Light Beyond*, 6, 12-13; Ring, *Heading*, 317, 318, 323, 329.
61. Moody, *The Light Beyond*, 193.
62. Ibid., 197.
63. Cf. Tal Brooke, *Riders of the Cosmic Circuit*, available from SCP, P.O. Box 4308, Berkeley, CA 94704.
64. Ring, *Heading*, 87, 99, 102-103, etc.
65. Ibid., 120.
66. Stanislav Grof, Book Review, *The Journal of Transpersonal Psychology*, Vol. 16, No. 2 (1984): 246.
67. Ring, *Heading*, 51.
68. Ibid., Chs. 4–8.
69. Ibid., 87-88.
70. John Pennachio, "Near-Death Experiences as Mystical Experience," *Journal of Religion and Health*, Vol. 25, No. 1 (1986): 64, 70-71.
71. Tillman Rodabough, "Near-Death Experiences: An Examination of the Supporting Data and Alternative Explanations," *Death Studies*, Vol. 9, No. 2 (1985): 102-103.
72. R.K. Siegel and A.E. Hirschman, "Hashish Near-Death Experience," *Anabiosis*, Vol. 4, No. 1 (Spring 1984): 69, 84-85.
73. John Weldon, *Yoga* unpublished ms., cf. Ankerberg and Weldon, *Can You Trust Your Doctor?* Ch. 19.
74. Ring, *Heading*, 231 (emphasis added).
75. Ibid., 234.
76. Ibid., 237.
77. See *Anabiosis*, Vol. 4, Nos. 1 & 2; Vol. 3, No. 1; Vol. 5, No. 2.
78. Ring, *Heading*, 226.
79. Ibid., 227-228.
80. Ibid., 87-88.
81. Tal Brooke, *Riders*, passim; cf. Ankerberg and Weldon, *Can You Trust Your Doctor?* Ch. 19.
82. Ring, *Heading*, 89; cf. 90-219.
83. C.R. Lundahl and H.A. Widdison, "The Mormon Explanation of Near-Death Experiences," *Anabiosis*, Vol. 3, No. 1 (June 1983): 103; cf. John Ankerberg and John Weldon, *Everything You Ever Wanted to Know About Mormonism* (Eugene, OR: Harvest House, 1992), Chs. 18-20 and C.R. Lundahl, "The Perceived Otherworld in Mormon Near-Death Experiences As Social and Physical Description," *Omega*, Vol. 12, 319-327 (1981-82); Leon Rhodes, "The NDE Enlarged by Swedenborg's Vision," *Anabiosis*, Vol. 2, No. 1 (June 1992): 15ff.; Carl Becker (Osaka University, Osaka, Japan), "Views from Tibet: NDEs and the Book of the Dead," who draws many parallels between the death-bed visions in the Tibetan Bon religion and Vajrayana (tantric) Buddhism as found in the *Tibetan Book of the Dead*.
84. Kenneth Ring, "From Alpha to Omega: Ancient Mysteries and the Near-Death Experience," *Anabiosis*, Vol. 5, No. 2 (1986): 8-9.
85. Ibid., 4.
86. Lennie Kronish, "Elisabeth Kubler-Ross: Messenger of Love," *Yoga Journal* (September/October 1976): 18-20; Elisabeth Kubler-Ross, *Death: The Final Stage of Growth* (New Jersey: Prentice Hall, 1975), 119; K. Coleman, "Elisabeth Kubler-Ross in the Afterword of Entities," *New West* (July 30, 1979).

87. Moody, *Life After Life*, 9.

88. Archie Matson, *Afterlife* (New York: Harper & Row, 1977), 35, 57, 73, 92.

89. Harold Sherman, *You Live After Death* (New York: Fawcett, 1972), 156; seven other examples are cited in Weldon and Levitt, *Is There Life After Death?* Ch. 5, notes.

90. John Ankerberg and John Weldon, *The Dangers of the Occult: Some Consequences of the Modern Search for Enlightenment* [tentative title] (Eugene, OR: Harvest House, 1993), unpublished ms.

91. Ring, *Heading*, 226.

92. Ibid., 145-146.

93. Ibid., 158.

94. Ibid., 160.

95. Ian Stevensen, *Twenty Cases Suggestive of Reincarnation*, 374-377; John Weldon, *Reincarnation*, unpublished ms., passim; Robert Morey, *Reincarnation and Christianity*, 30; Geisler and Amano, *The Reincarnation Sensation*, 78-82; John Snyder, *Reincarnation Vs. Resurrection*, 88-90; Mark Albrecht, *Reincarnation: A Christian Appraisal*, 71.

96. Ring, *Heading*, 57-58, 153.

97. Ibid., 62.

98. Ibid., 220.

99. Ibid., 151.

100. Ibid.

101. Ibid., 145-146.

102. Ibid., 87.

103. The biblical God is personal (John 12); He is Holy and hates evil (Habakkuk 1:13; Proverbs 6:16); He is the Creator of the Universe (Genesis 1:1); All religions do not worship the same God (John 14:6; Acts 4:12).

104. Moody, *The Light Beyond*, 27.

105. Robert Kastenbaum, *Is There Life After Death?* (New York: Prentice Hall, 1984), 25; citing G.A. Garfield in Kastenbaum, ed., *Between Life and Death* (New York: Spring Publishers, 1979), 54-55.

106. E.g., see Robert Gram, *An Enemy Disguised* (New York: Nelson, 1985).

107. For examples see Ankerberg, *Cult Watch*, 101, 286.

108. Ring, *Heading*, 93.

109. Ibid., 91.

110. Kenneth Ring and Stephen Franklin, "Do Suicide Survivors Report Near-Death Experiences?" in Craig R. Lundahl, *A Collection of Near-Death Research Readings*, from K.J. Drab, Book Review, *Anabiosis*, Vol. 3, No. 1: 110.

111. Morse, *Closer*, 177-179; Ring, *Heading*, 126, 179.

112. Ring, *Heading*, 94-98.

113. Ibid., 96.

114. Matthew 17:18; Nandor Fodor, *Encyclopaedia of Psychic Science* (Secaucus, NJ: Citadel, 1974), 234.

115. Cf. Ankerberg and Weldon, *Dangers*; Johanna Michaelsen, *Like Lambs to the Slaughter* (Eugene, OR: Harvest House, 1989).

116. Morse, *Closer*, 77-82.

117. Ibid., 92-93, 131, 126, 149, 163.

118. Cited respectively in Morse, *Closer*, 7, 122-123, 124, 131-132, 145-146, 148-149, 152-154, 155-156, 157-158.

119. Moody, *The Light Beyond*, 59.

120. Morse, *Closer*, 164-165.

121. Ibid., 151, 163.

122. Ibid.

123. Conditionalists variously assert a resurrection prior to annihilation; nevertheless, there is no resurrection to eternal life.

124. Georgine Milmine, *The Life of Mary Baker G. Eddy and the History of Christian Science* (Grand Rapids: Baker, 1971 rpt.), 28-31, 66-67, 111-116.

125. Mary Baker Eddy, *Science and Health with Key to the Scriptures* (Boston: First Church of Christ Scientist, 1971), 429.

126. Mary Baker Eddy, *Unity of Good* (Boston: Trustees Under the Will of Mary Baker Eddy, 1908), 3.

127. *Questions and Answers on Christian Science* (Boston: Christian Science Publishing Company, 1974), 6.

128. Edgar Cayce, *A Search for God*, Book 2 (Virginia Beach: ARE Study Group, 1975), 64 (*Reading*, No. 262-73); Book 1: 13.

129. Sun Myung Moon, "The Master Speaks," No. 4: 1 (Xerox copy of transcribed lecture).

130. Joseph Talmage, *A Study of the Articles of Faith* (Salt Lake City: Church of Jesus Christ of Latter-day Saints, 1976), 61.

131. David John Hill, *Is There a Real Hellfire?* (Pasadena, CA: Ambassador College Press, 1974), 20, 42.

132. Watchtower Bible and Tract Society, *Is This Life All There Is?* (Brooklyn: WBTS, 1974), 96.

133. Emanuel Swedenborg, *The True Christian Religion*, Vol. 2, No. 652 (Swedenborg Foundation, 1771), 183.

48

134. Darwin Gross, *Your Right to Know* (Menlo Park, CA: Illuminated Way Press, 1979), 26.
135. Paul Twitchell, *Eckankar: The Key to Secret Worlds* (New York: Lancer, 1969), 240; *Eck World News* (March 1976): 4.
136. Charles Fillmore, *Dynamics for Living* (Lee's Summit, MO: Unity Books, 1967), 278-279.
137. Mark and Elizabeth Prophet, *Climb the Highest Mountain* (Los Angeles: Summit University Press, 1977), 349.
138. N.a., "What Is Death?" (London: The Dawn Book Supply, 1971), 9; cf. Robert Roberts, *Christendom Astray* (Birmingham, England: The Christadelphian, 1969), 99.
139. The Christadelphians, *A Declaration of the Truth Revealed in the Bible* (South Australia: Logos, n.d.), 44.
140. Alice A. Bailey, *Esoteric Healing* (New York: Lucis Press, 1977), 442.
141. David Berg, "Out of This World" (November 25, 1977), GP686, 131, 133, 138. (tract)
142. Fannie James, *Selected Bible Readings* (Denver: First Divine Science Church, 1962), 143; Irwin Gregg, *The Divine Science Way* (Denver: Divine Science Federation Int'l., 1975), 168.
143. Max Heindel, *The Rosicrucian Cosmo-Conception* (Oceanside, CA: The Rosicrucian Fellowship, 1977), 229-230.
144. H. Spencer Lewis, *Mansions of the Soul: The Cosmic Conception* (San Jose, CA: AMORC, 1977), 301-302.
145. W. Argow, "Unitarian Universalism: Some Questions Answered" (Boston: October 1978), 8 (UUA pamphlet).
146. *Fundamental Group Outline: Eighth Class* (Santa Fe: St. Germaine Press, 1973), 16.
147. Godfre Ray King, *The Magic Presence* (Santa Fe: St. Germaine Press, 1974), 176-177.
148. H.P. Blavatsky, *The Key to Theosophy* (London: Theosophical, 1968), 110.
149. Theosophical Society of America, "When Death Occurs" (pamphlet) (Wheaton, IL: TSA, n.d.), 13.
150. J.Z. Knight, *Ramtha Voyage to the New World* (New York: Ballentine, 1987), 62, 252.
151. Ruth Montgomery, *A World Beyond* (Greenwich, CT: Fawcett Cress, 1972), 66; Ruth Montgomery, *Here and Hereafter* (Greenwich, CT: Fawcett Cress, 1968), 174.
152. E.g., Advent Christians, Seventh-day Adventists and some leading evangelicals, cf. Kenneth Kantzer and Carl F. Henry, eds., *Evangelical Affirmations* (Grand Rapids: Zondervan, 1990), 124.
153. Carl G. Johnson, *Hell You Say?* (Newtown, PA: Timothy Books, 1974).
154. Conversation between Dr. Walter Kaiser and John Ankerberg, 1991, citing Dr. Hunter; cf. Alan W. Gnomes, "Evangelicals and the Annihilation of Hell," *Christian Research Journal*, Part 1 (Spring 1991) and Part 2 (Summer 1991).
155. J.I. Packer in *Christianity Today* (January 17, 1986).
156. D.B. Eller, "Universalism," in Walter Elwell, ed., *Evangelical Dictionary of Theology* (Grand Rapids: Baker, 1984), 1130.
157. Stephen H. Travis, *Christian Hope and the Future* (Downers Grove, IL: InterVarsity, 1980), 118.
158. Vernon C. Grounds, "The Final State of Wicked," *Journal of the Evangelical Theological Society*, Vol. 24, No. 3 (September 1981): 211.
159. Richard J. Bauckham, "Universalism: A Historical Survey," *Themelios*, Vol. 4, No. 2 (January 1979): 48.
160. Arthur Conan Doyle, *The New Revelation*, 1919, from Johnson, *Hell*, 106.
161. Robert A. Morey, *Death and the Afterlife* (Minneapolis: Bethany, 1984), 230-231.
162. Martin, *Hostage*, 482.
163. John Weldon, "New Age Intuition," and "Self Help Therapy: Inner Guides and Imagination as Personal Healers," unpublished ms.
164. Harold O.J. Brown, *The Protest of a Troubled Protestant* (New Rochelle, NY: Arlington House, 1969), 213.
165. C.S. Lewis, *The Great Divorce* (New York: MacMillan, 1946), 69.
166. C.S. Lewis, *The Problem of Pain* (New York: MacMillan, 1971), 118-119.
167. Detailed refutations of unorthodox views relating to scriptural arguments, interpretation and biblical words are found in Morey's *Death and the Afterlife*.
168. J.I. Packer, "Evangelicals and the Way of Salvation," in Kantzer & Henry, eds., *Evangelical Affirmations*, 110.
169. Taken from John Stott, *Becoming a Christian* (Downers Grove, IL: InterVarsity, 1950), 25-26.